Who Is She Now?

Also by Kerry O'Regan and published by Ginninderra Press
The Things My Best Friends Told Me for the Camino and for Life

Kerry O'Regan

Who Is She Now?

Who Is She Now?
ISBN 978 1 76041 272 2
Copyright © Kerry O'Regan 2017

First published 2017 by
Ginninderra Press
PO Box 3461 Port Adelaide 5015 Australia
www.ginninderrapress.com.au

Contents

The child that was	7
Earliest memory	9
Bride and groom	10
A swing called Dobbin	13
First days at school	15
Easter I	17
The Story of Sin and Souls	18
Games we place	22
First Communion	24
Christmas I	27
My brother Michael	30
Altar boys	34
My sister Maureen	39
School milk	41
Elocution lessons	42
Childhood chores I	45
The front path	46
How long is half a log?	48
The things I envy	51
Washday Bedtime	54
How to become a saint	55
Banks Street Buses	57
Yes, Mum	59
Doing what I'm told	61
Friday Lessons	63
Martha and Mary, Mum and me	64
The School Inspector	65
A Message for Life	68
Just Mum	69
Holiday Stories	70

Childhood chores II	72
A birthday surprise	74
Four sisters	75
Easter II	76
Them	80
I hate wind, Mum says	81
Childhood chores III	82
A parental duet	84
Christmas II	85
The times are a-changing	87

The child that was

Father of the man
they say.
Perhaps also
Mother of the woman
though they don't say that.
I look at the child
The little one.
The dear little one.
The child that I once was.
And I wonder. Ponder.
I gaze on the fragments of memories
Like leafing through an old photo album
with most pages missing.
Or viewing reels of old film
mostly erased.
Funny thing
memory.
The bits that stay
and the bits that go.
I gaze on these things
and wonder
at the mothering
the birthing
of the me
that is.
A young boy I knew
once looked at a photo
of a child
and asked
Who is that?

When told
That was your uncle when he was a little boy
asked
profoundly
Well, who is it now?
I gaze on the memories I carry
of the child I was
Those faded photos.
Those fragments of film that remain
And I ask
Who is she now?

Earliest memory

I am very small.
Not sure how old.
Young enough to be stricken
by irrational fear.
Any age up to ninety
you say.
You could be right.
I stand
alone
and look up
at the leadlight door
at the end of the hall.
It's been there all my life
Harmless enough.
Unnoticed even.
Most people see it as a rose
Shades of pink
Some green.
Today
for me
it is an eye. A giant eye.
Looking. At me.
Evil and menacing
in its intent.
I scream in terror.
The things we turn into monsters.

Bride and groom

I'm now three years old
Three and a half actually.
I know
because it says in the newspaper clipping
that Mum cuts out
and keeps.
Margaret from next door
and I
go to a fancy dress ball.
Margaret is just three
the paper says.
We go as a bride and groom.
She is the bride
and wears a white lacy dress
and a veil
and has her hair curled.
I am the groom.
I wear a black suit
and white shirt
with a bow tie
and have my hair tucked
under my hat.
I don't mind being the groom
who wears a top hat.
We don't have a top hat
so they make one
Dad and the older kids
from a cornflakes packet.
Cut it out and paint it black.

It looks just like a real one
and they tuck my hair under it
so I look like a proper groom.
I have black shoes
but no black socks
So they blacken my feet with a cork
which may have been burnt
or maybe black with boot polish.
It makes my feet black enough
the bits that show.
We go to a big hall
and walk around in a circle
with the others in fancy dress.
I don't much notice the others
what they are wearing
Maybe some nursery rhyme characters.
I notice the tiny tiles on the floor.
Little black and white tiles set in big swirly patterns.
We win first prize
Margaret and I.
She in her lacy dress
me in my top hat
made from a cornflakes packet
and my blackened feet.
They take our photo and put it in the paper.
My bow tie all askew
and the black on one foot just starting to smear off
if you look carefully enough.

We look scared. And solemn. Very solemn.
As solemn as my parents look
in their wedding photo.
Perhaps they were scared too.

A swing called Dobbin

It's strange perhaps
for a swing to have a name.
Our swing is called Dobbin.
It may have started life as a swinging horse
So of course it needed a name.
Mr Swenson from over the back
made it.
Swensons have two horse swings
that you sit on
astride.
They have flat heads
like hobby horses.
Handles to hold
but no stick that drags.
Ropes instead
that hang from the floor
of their high Queensland house.
You sit astride these horses
these horses with heads
and swing
backwards and forwards.
Swenson's swings don't have names.
Dobbin has no head
if it ever did
though it still has a name.
It didn't lose that.

We don't sit astride our swing
our swing called Dobbin.
We sit the other way.
Sideways.
And swing it sideways.
A few of us at a time
if we want.
Mum swings there with us
and sings.
Sings to the back and forth
rhythm of the swing
that was once a horse
perhaps.
My big sisters swing with me too
at bedtime.
They sing as well.
Lullabies or hymns or popular songs
until I'm lulled to sleep
by the rhythm and the singing and the love.
We kids swing on Dobbin
as part of our play.
We sing too.
Pop songs or oldies
carols at Christmas time.
We love our swing
called Dobbin
that may once have been
a horse.

First days at school

On my first day at school
I tell Sister Bride
that I can say the alphabet
forwards and backwards.
Sister Bride says nothing.
I don't tell her anything else.
We sit in rows
and chant from a chart
A like an apple on a twig
A says a
B like a bat and ball
B says b
And so on through the alphabet
that I know. Forwards and backwards.
We are given lumps of grey plasticine.
Perhaps not always grey. Once different colours
but now sludgy grey.
We can roll it into sausages and balls. Make things.
We do it on a special piece of lino
so it won't stick to the desk.
Mine always sticks to the lino.
I don't know why.
I don't try to make it stick.
But it does. Always.
I'm not good at skipping.
The others laugh at that.
Gloria doesn't laugh.
Gloria has ringlets.

She says
in her kind soft voice
Don't cry, Kerry.
One day there is a mouse in my school bag.
I see it run out.
It nibbles at my lunch before it goes.
My bag smells of mouse.
My lunch smells of mouse.
I can't eat sandwiches smelling of mouse.
I feel sick. Mouse-lunch sick.
Sister Bride says Nonsense!
Stand there. Outside.
Until you eat your perfectly good lunch.
Schooldays. The happiest days of our lives.
They do get better.

Easter I

Easter means eggs.
Everyone knows that.
Made of hard candy
Pale pink or yellow. Mostly.
But where do they come from?
How do they get here?
Some say the Easter Bunny
like Santa at Christmas
comes to each house
leaving an egg for every child.
A pink or yellow candy egg.
My big brother Kevin says no.
Kevin is mathematical. Logical. Literal.
An engineer one day.
Kevin says no. That can't be.
Bunnies don't lay eggs.
Birds lay eggs.
There must be an Easter Bird.
So we make a nest
Kevin and I
at the end of my bed.
Gather up some old clothes,
make a nest
for the Easter Bird to lay its egg
its pink or yellow candy egg.
And yes. On Easter morning
there it is.
My pink or yellow candy egg
left in my nest
by the Easter Bird.
Of course.

The Story of Sin and Souls

One of the first things I learn at school
is that
'God made me
giving me a body and a soul.'
They tell us that the soul is that part of us that will live for ever
Where it will live
depending on its state of cleanliness
when we die.
Cleanliness being next to godliness
I guess.
It was meant to be bright and shiny
like a freshly scrubbed bathroom
(though they don't say that).
Stained already by Original Sin
like some of our tea-stained tablecloths
(they don't say that either).
That stain removed by baptism
at least in part
The new wonder-cleaner
(though they don't say…you get the idea).
Spotted by each sin, each transgression.
Small sins: small stains
removed by repentance, confession, penance.
Or in an emergency
heart attack, imminent plane crash
by the do-it-yourself stain remover
called An Act of Perfect Contrition
'Oh my God
I am heartily sorry
for having offended thee.'

Sometimes misheard or mistold by naughty older siblings as
'Partly sorry
For having a friend like thee.'
Big sins: big stains.
Die without the application of stain remover
and straight to hell for you
my girl.
Eternal wailing and gnashing of teeth
Not to mention the eternal flames
Worse than anything earth could offer.
Earthly stain removers
can only do so much.
Something always remains
however faintly.
Stains are only totally removed
by the New Improved
Cleansing Fires of Purgatory.
Soaked – no, seared –
for a short or long time
depending on
the severity of the stain.
Don't know how sentence-length works
in the timelessness of eternity.
But that is just one of the puzzles.
Once fully cleansed by Purgatory
out of jail free
and off to Heaven
for Eternal bliss.

Only those with perfectly stain-free souls
can go
straight to heaven.
The Blessed Virgin Mary
was the only one
in the whole history of humanity
(besides Jesus of course)
to be whooshed straight up to heaven
body *and* soul
without a whiff
of Purgatory flames.
The Immaculate Conception.
I could explain
but won't.
What of babies
not yet baptised
still carrying Original Sin
but otherwise stain-free?
Not heaven
that's for sure.
Not clean enough for that.
Not hell.
They've done no wrong themselves
(other than being born of Eve).
Purgatory won't do it
(for some reason).
We know.
Limbo
a place of eternal bliss. Almost perfect.

All the benefits of heaven
but without the presence of God.
Sorry, babies.
Not your fault.
So there it is
all neatly packaged.
No legal loopholes
(except maybe Indulgences
those get out of jail free cards
fully transferable –
but that's another story).
It all makes sense
For now.

Games we place

There's a grassy space
at the end of our dead-end street.
Belongs to no one
or everyone.
We call it
The Grass Outside Mason's.
We say to Mum
Can we go and play
on the Grass Outside Mason's?
She mostly says yes.
We play there together
all the neighbourhood kids.
We play
Red Rover
Statues
Roman soldiers
Tiggy
Farmer's in the Dell
Oranges and Lemons
When it's time
Mum calls us home.
Or Dad whistles
his special
Time to Come Home
whistle.
We don't want to go home.
Don't want to stop.
We say
Aw, Mum
Can't we play some more?

We're having such fun.
But Mum just says
It's always best
to stop
when the fun is at its height.
I don't believe that.
Not really.
Besides
how do you know
when the fun is at its height?

First Communion

When we are seven
we make our First Communion.
First Confession too.
We learn what we have to say:
'Bless me, Father, for I have sinned.
This is my first confession, Father,
and I accuse myself of…'
Then we have to tell our sins.
I worry about that
getting it right.
What sins have I committed?
What if I miss some?
Sister Bride gives us examples.
Being disobedient.
Yes to that. Sometimes.
Telling lies.
Have I?
Being mean, unkind.
To Michael I have.
I make my list. In my head.
We have to wear white dresses.
Mum makes me a new white dress
and Maureen embroiders flowers
on the collar.

We have to buy a white veil
and take it to school in plenty of time
so Sister Bride can make it right.
She sews it
so a little frill stands up
on top of our heads
like a turned-up baseball cap.
Elastic for under our chin
to keep our veil in place.
We practise
walking into the church
in lines
with our palms together
in front of us.
Thumbs crossed.
We file into the front pews
where we will sit
and then to the altar rails
where we will kneel
hands clasped
to receive Communion.
Our First Communion.
We practise until we know what to do.
Till we get it right.

One Sister tells us
that the Great Emperor Napoleon
said his First Communion Day
was the best day of his life.
We fast on our First Communion Day.
You must be fasting to receive Communion
I don't know why.
We line up outside the church.
The girls in their new white dresses.
White veils with the frill standing up
like the peak of a baseball cap.
White socks. Black shoes.
The boys with white shirts. Long sleeves.
Long socks. Pulled up.
We walk with our hands clasped
in lines
into the front pews.
We have practised enough
so we get it right
with our families there to watch.
After, there is a special breakfast.
We sit in the infants classroom
and have party food for breakfast.
After that
we can go to Confession and Communion
as often as we want.
As often as we should.
That is what we do now.

Christmas I

Two days before Christmas
Dad chops the head off
a couple of chooks.
He hangs them
by their scaly feet
upside down
from the clothesline
so the blood drains out.
Next day
Christmas Eve
Mum plucks them.
She sits
a big tub of hot water
between her legs.
She says
the hot water loosens the feathers.
She sits there
the tub between her legs
and pulls the feathers
from the chooks.
She sits there
sweating
as the feathers fly.
The feathers fly
into the tub
around the tub
onto her clothes
onto her hair
onto her arms
onto her face

where they stick
with the sweat
and the hot water.
Her busy, plucking hands
make the feathers fly
until the chooks are naked
and bare
except for the spots
the little lumps
where the feathers used to be.
She cuts off their scaly feet
slits the skin of their bare, naked bodies
and pulls out their insides.
She tells me what all the bits are.
The heart, the gut, the gizzard.
Funny word, gizzard.
She tells me what those bits did
yesterday
when the chooks were still pecking their way
around the chook yard
unaware of tomorrow's fate
Tomorrow's destiny.
Mum discards some of the innards
Other bits she chops up
Mixes them with breadcrumbs, onions, herbs
and puts it all back inside
sews up the slit
with string
and a big needle.

Ties the legs together.
Not that they'll run anywhere.
Not any more.
Not now.
She tucks the neck inside
the long, dangly neck
that now has no head.
And that's the chooks
all ready to cook
for Christmas.

My brother Michael

Michael is my little brother.
We squabble at times
as siblings do.
I do not know. Can not know.
that one day
sixty years from now
I will wake one morning
and think
Today is Michael's birthday
Or would have been.
A nice symmetry to that.
The year split in half. Neatly.
Between birthday and Christmas.
Does he like that?
The way his birthday and Christmas
split the year in half?
I don't know.
So much I don't know.
We are the babies
he and I.
Straggling at the end
of our big straggling family.
The little ones.
Spoilt, they say.
Certainly loved.
Cosseted. Played with. Wondered at.
Enfolded in the magic.
Not peas in a pod
Michael and I.
More like yin and yang.

I the clever little one.
He the cute one.
I the thinker.
He the doer.
School is a breeze.
For me.
Not for him.
One nun says
Why can't you be like your sister?
How cruel.
He says nothing. I say nothing.
So much unsaid.
Mum sits with him each afternoon.
Going over and over.
Patiently. Persistently.
The way words work.
And numbers.
The unfathomable mystery of it all.
So hard for him.
Life's not fair.
I will stay with my books.
Diligent. Studious.
Michael will do stuff.
Play sport. Drive trucks.
Go to war.
But mostly he will drive a tiny green car
with a big, long surfboard on top.
Each weekend. With his mates.
Off to the coast.
Michael off fighting the waves.

And winning.
But one day he doesn't win.
They do.
He will go into the waves.
ad not come out.
Not alive.
Good way to die perhaps.
For him.
But no notice.
No goodbyes.
No time, no chance, to say
what hasn't been said.
He doesn't ever say
I resent what you have. What you are.
I don't think he does. Resent it.
He doesn't say
I am proud of you
my clever big sister.
Though I think he is. Proud.
I don't say
I love your gentle soul
your generous spirit
that doesn't ask
Why you?
Why me?

I will say it then
sixty years from now
on his birthday
I will wake and say
Michael, my dear little brother
I am proud of you
I love you.
I don't know that now
Or perhaps I would say. Would do.
Something.

Altar boys

I want to be an altar boy.
Some kids get to be an altar boy.
Some boys.
Girls can't.
We're not allowed.
Altar boys wear long black gowns
shorter white gowns
over the top.
They help the priest say the Mass.
Hover round the altar
with the priest
just a bit lower down.
They wear their gowns.
Clasp their hands
as in prayer.
Look down.
Walk carefully.
Do important things.
They look holy.
Look important.
Look close to God.
I want to do that.
Before Mass starts
they come to the altar
with a long stick
taper on the end
and light the candles
high on the altar.
One by one.
I'd like to do that.

Sometimes one doesn't light
I want to call out
Hey, you missed one.
But you can't do that
Not in church.
They notice anyway
and come back.
Make sure all the candles are lit.
They help the priest
say the prayers of the Mass
Kyrie eleison
Christe eleison
Confetior deo omnipotenti
I'd like to do that
Say those Latin prayers
Up there with the priest.
They carry things around. Important things.
Bread and wine
for the Offertory
water and a tiny white cloth
for the priest to wash his hands.
Before Communion
they toss the long white cloth
over the altar rails.
The cloth that hangs
like a curtain
against the rails.
They cover the rails
for us to rest our hands on
to receive Communion.

Like the way you toss a sheet
over the end of the bed
when you're making it.
Sometimes
we pretend to be altar boys
when we're making the bed.
Tossing the sheet
the way they toss the altar rail cloth.
Sometimes
we pretend to be Father Bolton.
The way he throws back his head
his bald priestly head
and wags it from side to side
as he says his prayers
in Latin.
We don't know the Latin
so we just say
'Lal lal lal lal lal'
in our father bolton voice
as we throw back our heads
and wag them from side to side.
And then we giggle
at our naughtiness.
It is naughty
to make fun of anyone
especially priests and nuns.
'God's own holy people'
my grandma used to call them
so I'm told.

I probably should tell it
in Confession
But I don't.
I can't tell a priest
in Confession
Bless me, Father
I made fun of you
I threw back my head
and wagged it
from side to side
and giggled.
I can't say that.
At Communion
the altar boy
holds a little brass tray
under our chin
while the priest
places the host
on our tongue.
To catch any crumbs
I suppose
or in case the priest misses.
Can't have bits
of the Body of Christ
falling on the floor.
After Mass
the altar boys
come back again
with their long sticks
with a little brass cone on the end.

They use those
to put out the candle flames.
I would like to do that.
I would like to be an altar boy
but I can't.
Girls are not allowed.

My sister Maureen

Maureen is my biggest sister
She is beautiful
Very beautiful
Even I can see that.
I love to sit on the bed
and watch her
dress for a ball
like Cinderella
turning into
the beautiful princess.
The hair. The dress. The make-up.
A fairy tale
being lived out
before my eyes.
Maureen sings.
We all sing. Well, almost all.
The rest of us
just open our mouths
and out it comes
one way or another.
But Maureen has lessons.
Sings properly
in competitions and shows
Sometimes Clare takes us to see the shows
Michael and me.
There's one song Maureen sings
that is so sad.
Thou art lost to me forever
Will I never see thee more?

Oh what grief
Past belief
She is gone whom I adore
She is gone whom I adore
Euridice. Euridice.
I cry
when Maureen sings that song
I feel the sadness go somewhere deep inside of me.
It's too sad for me
I say
Maureen doesn't stop
and neither do I.
She keeps on singing
and I keep on weeping
at the song
that is
too sad.

School milk

Someone
the government probably
has decided to make us healthy
by sending to the school
little bottles of milk
one for each of us
every day
for us to drink.
A big truck
brings the crates of milk
some time after nine.
And they sit there
on those hot Queensland mornings
until Little Lunch
at eleven.
The milk is never cold
by Little Lunch time.
Just slightly warm
after sitting there
waiting for us
in the heat.
We drink the milk
the government has sent us.
Those slightly warm
little bottles of milk.
Then we rinse our bottles
and place them back in the crates
for the men to collect
tomorrow
when they bring us more bottles
of slightly warm milk
to make us healthy.

Elocution lessons

Mrs Hansen comes each week
for elocution lessons.
Mrs Hansen is not a Catholic
but each week when she comes
we stand and chant
in unison
in our sing-song way
'Good morning Mrs Hansen
God bless you Mrs Hansen.'
That's what you do
at a Catholic school.
Mrs Hansen teaches us special rhymes
Exercises
Like 'The rain in Spain'.
So we speak with nice round vowels
and clear crisp consonants.
We learn poems we recite together
as a verse-speaking choir.
Our choir always comes first
in the eisteddfod
With our nice round vowels
and our clear crisp consonants
and our good expression.
Mrs Hansen tests our reading
come end of term.
We stand and read aloud
a paragraph or two from our reader.
Mrs Hansen tells us which bit to read.
She tells us our mark.
Something out of ten.

I like reading aloud.
So does Julie Foster.
Julie Foster is a poor kid.
Old tumbledown house.
No dad. Lots of kids.
Hair cut straight around just under her ears.
Collar. Neck. Fingernails.
Not always clean.
Julie Foster always gets 10 for reading.
Most kids don't.
Some never get anything very much.
I try not to look at them. Listen to them.
as they stand. And try. Very quietly
to say the words, those mysterious words
that are on the page.
They never get 10
or even 6.
But they still have to stand
and read
very quietly
in front of the class
and be told their score.
Their mark out of ten.
Like Noreen
who mumbles quietly. Inaudibly.
Imagined words.
And bites her lip.
And looks afraid.
We don't all learn to read. Not well

But we all learn to speak
Recite our poems
With nice round vowels
and clear crisp consonants.
Imagine
a whole school
of little Pygmalions.

Childhood chores I

The baker calls each day
bringing bread in a big wicker basket.
Not wrapped. Not sliced.
Just plain fresh loaves. In his basket.
Brown or white.
Not on weekends though
So come Monday
no more bread.
Or, what there is, stale.
Good enough for toast. For breakfast.
But not for sandwiches. Not for lunches.
So one of us, or two
must go to the bakery
nearly as far as school.
We walk
or ride a bike if we're big enough
to the bakery
with its freshly baked bread
and bring home a loaf
for lunches.
With maybe just a couple of bits
quite small bits really
of that freshly baked bread
pulled off and eaten
on that long, hungry walk home.

The front path

There's a concrete path
from the house
to the front gate.
It's good for games. Some games.
Just us.
Or the neighbourhood kids.
Skipping is one.
You tie the rope
one end
to the gate.
Someone holds the other end
turns the rope
while the rest skip.
One by one
or all in together
Salt and Pepper.
Other games
we chant to
as we skip.
There's soft stones
in the garden.
You can use these
to draw on the path.
It's OK to do that.
We're allowed to draw on the path
with the soft stones
from the garden.
Sometimes
we draw the outline for hopscotch.

Then we use the stone
to throw into the square
you hop around.
A different square each time
until you've done them all.
Or you can draw pictures
with the stones.
The path is marked into squares
so we can each have a square
to draw our own picture
with a soft stone
from the garden.
The pictures wear away
or wash away
soon enough
ready for next time.
The front path
is a good place
to play games.
Skipping and hopping and drawing.

How long is half a log?

Next door
there's always been
a vacant block.
We like to play there.
Make tunnels and cubbies
in the lantana.
But one day
a man starts to build a real house there
out of wood.
A cheerful man
called Leo Malone
who whistles while he works
with his hammer
hanging from his belt.
We are told
not to play there now
in that house
Leo is building.
But we do anyway. It's fun.
Climbing around
in the wooden frame
Leo is turning into a house.
One day
I step on a plank
that's not nailed down.
The plank and I
go crashing to the ground.
I fall face down
onto half a log.

That is important. The half-log bit.
I break my arm.
Not badly.
And smash my face
into the half-log.
Bruised, swollen, painful.
They take a photo
so I won't forget.
I don't forget.
They think it's funny
the grown-ups.
Not the damage. Not the breaks and bruises.
But the half-a-log part of the story.
They don't understand.
It's important to get it right.
Each time they tell the story
they say
Kerry fell through the half-made floor
onto a log below.
I correct them
and say
No. I fell onto half a log.
They think that's funny
I can tell.
But they don't understand.
They think that half a log
is like
half a piece of string.
I'm not silly.

I know that logs
like pieces of string
come in all sizes.
But if you took a piece of string
and split it in half
lengthwise
you'd have
half a piece of string
however long it was.
That's what half a log means.
That's what they don't get.
That's what I can't explain.
Sometimes
grown-ups
just don't understand.

The things I envy

At first
I envy the kids with slate sponges.
We learn to write on slates
with special slate pencils.
And we wash our slates clean
to use them again.
Some of us use old rags
But some kids
have a special little sponge.
Some even have
a special tin
to put it in.
I envy those.
Then I envy the girls who have
wooden pencil cases.
Especially the double-decker ones
that swivel
and have a lid
that slides
and lots of compartments
for pencils, rubbers, pencil sharpeners,
Special things.
Or have lids
that roll away somewhere
and have
lots of coloured pencils.
Long ones.
Mum always buys me
a packet of six.
Short ones.

I envy girls who have dolls.
One day I tell Santa Claus
I would like a doll for Christmas
One that can close its eyes.
And on Christmas morning
there she is.
My very own doll
that can close its eyes.
With a lavender dress.
I want to call her Rose.
Dad says
How about Mary
after the Mother of God.
Mum says
Well then, why not Rosemary.
One day
Rosemary disappears.
I am sad about that.
Mum says
I probably left her downstairs
and one of those poor kids took it
on their way through our yard
on the shortcut to the shops.
I envy the kids who have fruit and cake
with their lunch.
Not just sandwiches.
And bring their lunch in tins with pictures on the lid
not just wrapped in paper.
I envy the girls who learn piano.

One day at singing
the nun stops
and says to me
You have a very good ear.
You should learn piano.
I tell Mum I'd like to learn piano.
She says we can't afford it.
I'm sad about that.
That's about it.
The things I envy.

Washday Bedtime

Monday is washday.
Of course
sheets are washed. And pyjamas.
Besides everything else.
Sometimes
in winter
our flannelette pyjamas don't dry.
Not properly.
So Mum puts them in the oven. For a bit.
In the big baking dish used for Sunday roasts.
Not for too long. Or they'll scorch.
How nice it is
to put on clean warm pyjamas
fresh from the oven.
The other good thing about washday
is Mum making the bed
on top of you.
You lie on the bed
bottom sheet already tucked in
and she spreads the clean top sheet
over you
as you lie on the bed
in your clean warm pyjamas.
Then the blankets.
Then the bedspread.
All placed on top of you
while you lie there
on the bed.
Washday bedtime is the best.

How to become a saint

Sister Bergman
(is that her name?)
loves to tell
of little Maria Goretti.
Sister Bergman's eyes and voice go soft
as she reads us
again
her favourite story
of her favourite saint.
Maria was eleven
Just like us.
Alessandro was older
A young man.
He wanted Maria to consent
to impure acts.
Maria refused.
It was a mortal sin
Maria said.
But one day
when they were alone
Alessandro insisted.
Maria refused
maintaining her most precious
virginal purity.
Alessandro was furious.
Grabbed a knife
and stabbed her.
Fourteen times.
She died of course.
A martyr.

Her body violated
by the knife.
But her purity intact.
That's what made her a saint.

Banks Street Buses

To get to our place
you turn down Banks Street
past Newmarket State School
on the other side.
After a bit
there's stairs
you can walk up
to keep going
up the big hill
that Banks Street becomes.
But you don't do that.
Not to get to our place.
Instead
you take the tiny path
just wide enough for one person
around the end of Alexanders' place.
That takes you to our place
just across the road
second from the end.
12 Gosman Street.
Some people go up the stairs
And up the big hill
that Banks Street becomes
if they live up there.
Buses go up the hill.
Not up the stairs of course.
They groan and struggle
their way up that big hill.
Changing gears perhaps.

I don't know enough about buses
to know what that moment is.
That moment in their struggle
when something changes.
That moment
when something bad might happen.
Every time that happens
that moment of struggle.
Every time
At that moment of change
when I'm walking on the path
before you get to the stairs
and a bus is struggling and groaning
its way up the hill above
there's a bad thing I fear will happen.
I fear that the bus will lose its struggle with the hill.
That it will come hurtling back down
out of control
faster and faster
and crash onto me
as I walk on the path below
as I walk on that bit of path
just before the stairs.
It hasn't happened yet.
But each time I walk that path
on my way home
and a bus struggles and groans
and somehow pauses
on its way up Banks Street hill
I fear that it will.

Yes, Mum

I am impatient.
I want it to be
next week
holidays
Christmas
my birthday
when I'm grown-up.
Mum smiles
and says
in her calm gentle way
Now is the best time.
I don't believe her
But I tuck it away
somewhere
until
the time when I am ready to believe it.
Or almost ready.
I am impatient.
We're a huggy kind of family
Mum will hug us
just for a minute
just in passing.
But today I'm impatient.
I'm too busy.
No time for that sort of thing.
Not now. Not today.
She says
in that way of hers.
There's always time for a little love and affection.

I am impatient.
At odds with the world.
Nothing is right.
Mum says
Why don't you sing a little song?
I am impatient. Petulant.
I stamp my foot
at least metaphorically.
I don't feel like singing.
She says
You don't sing because you're happy;
You're happy because you sing.
She's right
of course.

Doing what I'm told

Old Mr Ross sits at the top of his stairs
just inside his front door.
One day
when I'm walking past
he's standing there
at the top of his stairs.
He holds up a tennis ball
and beckons me to come
and take the ball.
It's an old tennis ball
with a red mark on it.
I do not want to go up Mr Ross's stairs
up to his front door
to take his tennis ball
with the red mark on it.
Across the road
Mrs Swenson waters her garden.
'Mr Ross wants to give you the tennis ball'
she says.
'Go on. Go and get it.'
I am a good little girl
so I do as I'm told.
Though I don't want to.
I don't want to go up the stairs
to where Mr Ross is standing
just inside his front door.
But I go.
I do as I am told.

I go up Mr Ross's stairs
to where he is standing
just inside his front door.
Mr Ross closes the door.
He sits on the chair in front of me.
I look at Mr Ross's white hair.
I look at the yellow-brown stain
in his white moustache.
Mum has told us
not to let anyone touch
our private parts.
She didn't tell us
how to stop someone
doing that.
She didn't tell us
what we should do then.
I go back down Mr Ross's stairs.
I leave the tennis ball behind.
The old tennis ball
with the red mark on it.
Mrs Swenson is still
watering her garden.
I don't tell her
what Mr Ross just did.
I don't tell Mum
what Mr Ross did.
I don't tell anyone
what Mr Ross did.
Not for a long time.

Friday Lessons

Every Friday morning
after prayers
we have a Chocolate Wheel.
The big boys run it.
They sell us the 'bats'
Wooden slats with numbers. Painted on.
We can buy a bat for a penny.
When all the bats are sold
the boys spin the wheel.
When it stops
the one with that number
wins a prize.
We hand the bats back
and try again.
We keep going
until Sister runs out of prizes
or we run out of money.
One of our Friday lessons is
gambling.

Martha and Mary, Mum and me

I am sick a lot.
One of those childhood things
No one knows why
You wouldn't think so
looking at me later.
A lonely thing for a child. Being sick.
Lonely and scary.
What I want most on bad days
is for Mum to sit beside me.
Just sit.
Not say anything or do anything.
Not talk. Or read. Or tell stories.
Not sing even.
Just sit there and hold my hand.
I can see the Martha in her tugging at the Mary.
(The way it does.)
Come on. Come on. We have work to do.
(She does have eight other children
and a husband.)
I can see that, but I don't care.
I just want her to be there.
With me.
Holding my hand.
And she does.
For a while.

The School Inspector

The inspector comes to school
The nuns all breathless and smiling
We on Our Best Behaviour
like we've been told.
The inspector checks our books
Asks us questions
Gives us a sum to do.
Multiply £7/16/9 by 13
and convert your answer to pence.
We don't ask, don't think
Why would anyone want to do that?
It's just a sum we're told to do
So we do it. For the inspector.
I change it to pence first
then multiply by 13
That's easier.
After a while
the inspector tells us the answer.
I got it wrong.
He says everyone who got it wrong
should stand up.
I stand up
with the others
who got it wrong.
He says he'll work out the sum
on the board
and we should sit down
when we see what we did wrong.

He starts to multiply
£7/16/9 by 13.
Works it out
line by line.
Kids sit down
as they see where they went wrong
or sit down anyway.
I know
the inspector will not get
to where I went wrong
I didn't do it that way.
I don't know what to do.
I don't want to be standing there
by myself
at the end
because I couldn't see where I went wrong.
So I sit down
Some time.
The inspector finishes the multiplying
then converts to pence.
Gets the right answer.
Then he looks at us
and smiles.
He smiles like he's big
and important
and we're little
and not important.

He says
Now I'll show you something.
If you'd been smart
you'd have changed it to pence first
and then done the multiplying.
He shows us how to do it
the easy way. The smart way.
And smiles. His big important smile.
I don't say anything.
I can't say anything.
Not now. If I ever could.
But I smile. Secretly.
I feel pleased
I did it the smart way
though I got it wrong.
The inspector doesn't know.
No one else knows.
But I know.

A Message for Life

I bring home my test results
Mum asks
Was that the top mark?
No, I say, second.
Who got top?
I tell her
She says
'Fancy letting a boy beat you.'
I remember that
Absorb it into my being
Try not to let it happen again.

Just Mum

Sometimes there are
little clusters of women
from the church.
One of them
might ask
Are you the little O'Regan girl?
I say I am.
And then one will say
very seriously
Your mother's a wonderful woman.
And they'll look at each other
and nod. Seriously.
And not quite cluck their tongues.
I feel embarrassed.
What can they mean?
I love my mother. And all that.
But don't they know?
She's just our mum.
Just ordinary. Just everyday.
Just there. Being Mum.
Not what you'd nod together
and say 'wonderful' about.
Not what you'd almost cluck your tongues about.
She's just Mum.

Holiday Stories

It's nearly Christmas holidays
So Sister gathers us together
in the biggest classroom.
Just the older ones
Not the little ones
Not the infants.
Six weeks is a long time
for us to be good
without telling us.
Every day. How to be good.
So this has to be a big telling.
A serious telling. A scary telling.
We all squeeze together
in the big classroom
on a hot sticky Brisbane day
while Sister tells us
how to be good.
Or rather
what might happen
if we are not good.
She tells of the little girl
who rode her bike
instead of going to Mass one Sunday.
She fell off. Hit her head. Died.
Her Christmas presents forever unopened
in the bottom drawer.
She tells us of the little boy
who was too ashamed
to wear his brown scapula
into the sea.

He drowned.
We sit squeezed together
in the hot sticky room.
I feel the sweat trickle down the back of my legs.
Trickle down the back of my neck.
I feel the fear trickle down with it.
Sometimes at night
I lie awake
and feel that fear trickling down.
I don't want to fall off my bike
and die.
I don't want to go into the sea
and drown.
So I will try to be good.
I will try
to be good.

Childhood chores II

Washing the socks
that's the worst.
Or maybe
washing up after Sunday dinner.
Both happen on the weekend.
Both are bad.
Saturday morning.
A big pile of dirty, smelly, dark, thick, woolly
socks.
A big tub of water
a cake of soap
and just do it.
Even though the water gets darker and murkier as you go.
Every Sunday
brings
Sunday roast.
Meat. Three veg. Pudding.
Then
piles and piles
of greasy dishes.
No detergent
just soap fragments
in a little wire basket
that you shake in the water
in the hope
the unlikely hope
that it will outstrip the grease.
The grease always wins.

The mountain of greasy dishes
worse, of pots and pans,
never seems to lessen.
The water gets greasier.
Our reluctance gets greater.
Our pace gets slower.
The washing up spreads
interminably
into the afternoon.
Just sing while you do it
Mum says.
That always helps.
We try
in a half-hearted sort of way.
The grease remains.
Yes. They are the worst.

A birthday surprise

Dad gives me the money.
Mum has told him
she needs new petticoats
and her birthday's coming up.
Dad has taken the hint.
So he gives me the money
and says
Go and buy as much white lawn
as this will buy
for Mum's new petticoats.
Knowing no better
I take the money
and buy the lawn.
Lawn is cheap
so the money buys lots
of plain white lawn
for Mum's birthday surprise.
On the morning
she opens the parcel
quite a large parcel
smiles in her loving way
and says
Thank you, Hun.
Petticoats are just what I wanted.
Mum makes herself petticoats
with the plain white lawn.
Many petticoats.
She doesn't need new petticoats now.
Not for a long time.

Four sisters

I have four sisters.
There since my birth.
Bent over my cradle
like Sleeping Beauty's good fairies.
Keeping watch over the new precious one
that was me.
The one who almost wasn't.
Almost too small to be.
Small enough for doll's clothes.
These fairies brought their gifts.
The first brought beauty.
The aesthetics of life
of music, of art, of elegant ways.
The next brought love.
An honest practical love.
No frills, no highfaluts.
All-embracing, earth-mothering.
The third brought a wildness.
The thrill and the pain of being oneself
Of living, and loving, adventurously. Foolishly.
Whatever the cost.
The last, soul gifts
To ponder, to reflect
To know within one's heart.
They brought these gifts
those good fairies
to do with as I may.
I thank you, my sisters.

Easter II

I love Easter
The drama of it.
The story that's acted out.
We as observers and participants
like a Greek chorus.
All during Lent
the church statues are covered.
Shrouded in purple.
A sombre time.
People give things up.
Lollies. Sugar in their tea.
So life is sombre. Thoughtful.
Then Palm Sunday
The story is
that Jesus rides into Jerusalem
on a donkey.
The crowds welcome him
Wave palm fronds.
We take small pieces of palm.
Pine actually.
We hold them. Smell their pine fragrance.
We don't wave them.
But still, somehow
we are the welcoming crowds
acting out
that triumphant entry
into Jerusalem.
An ironic entry. As it turns out.
Lent continues. For another week.

Then Maundy Thursday
We read of the Last Supper.
The Agony. As it is called.
The request. The cry. The lament.
'Will you not watch one hour with me?'
We do. We watch. For that hour.
Not like the disciples
who all ran off.
The church is open all night
and people stay and watch.
Take turns. One after the other.
All through the night.
Watching. In silence
Answering that request.
One Easter
I go late at night
with my big brother Paul.
We watch together. In silence.
For that hour.
Read. Pray. Ponder.
We walk home in silence too.
Not wanting to. Not able to.
Let go its melancholy.
Good Friday
The drama more intense.
Statues still covered.
No flowers No candles.
The red sacristy lamp. Extinguished.
The tabernacle door wide open.

The tabernacle empty. Abandoned.
All emptiness and desolation.
At 3, the time of Jesus' death
people crowd into the church.
The priest reads the service.
Special. Unfamiliar. In Latin.
We can follow in English
though he tells us what to do
in Latin.
'*Levate.*' And we stand.
Somewhere in the service
it says
'Perfidious Jew.'
I wonder what that means
but forget to ask.
The priest walks around
the fourteen
Stations of the Cross
telling the story as he goes.
While we sit and kneel and stand
'*Levate*'
as we're told.
Following the drama.
Feeling the drama.
Feeling the sadness. The solemnity.
Of the crucifixion story.
Holy Saturday is like
an interval
in the drama.
A nothing day. A day of waiting.

But then Easter Day.
Maybe Midnight Mass
and the Pascal Candle.
All whiteness and brightness.
The Light of the World.
Flowers and candles.
Statues uncovered.
Alleluias ringing. Again and again.
Celebrating the resurrection.
The joy of it.
I love the drama
that is Easter.

Them

It's Them we have to worry about.
They're not PLU you know.
Not People Like Us.
I know who they are:
State School Kids.
The state school is nearby.
Just across the road. Almost.
Not good enough. Not for us.
We don our navy uniforms
black lace-up shoes
and walk the mile to our school.
St Ambrose's. The Catholic school.
We pass the others going the other way.
They wear ordinary clothes
sandals or bare feet.
(It is Queensland.)
We look down on that.
They say 'Catholic dogs jump like frogs
into holy water.'
What is our response? Our taunt.
Our definition of Other.
Something about Proddies.
Margaret Flay from next door
is my best friend
my constant playmate.
She is a State School Kid.
That's different.

I hate wind, Mum says

Mum hates the sound of wind.
Every windy night, she says
I hate wind.
One windy night, long ago, her little boy died.
Her precious one.
He died and the wind raged.
Elemental sorrow, like in Shakespeare.
The wind died; Brian died.
But his little grey fisher hat stayed, hanging behind the door.
Forlornly.
One day she could let go of that, that reminder.
But the wind won't let her forget.
It keeps coming back, the wind with its memories.
And each windy night, Mum says
I hate wind.
It was windy the night Brian died.

Childhood chores III

One job is
scrubbing the back stairs.
You need
a tub of water
a scrubbing brush
a bar of Velvet soap. Or Sunlight.
A cloth for rinsing.
You dip the brush into the water
Rub the soap on it.
And scrub. Make patterns.
Soapy lines with the bristles.
Side-to-side.
Up-and-down.
Zigzag.
Or swirly round-and-round designs.
And then you slosh it all off
with water and the cloth'
Like unraking a Zen garden
I suppose.
You get to know each step well
and find
each one is different
with its own personality
its own woody pattern.
Some flat
some shaped a little
through wear
or inclination.
Some move
just a bit.

Some rock solid.
I decorate each in a different way, with the brush and the soap
respecting their uniqueness
or relieving my own boredom. More like.
You have to find fun
where you can.
We don't scrub the wide front stairs
only the back ones.
I don't know why.

A parental duet

There are two refrains
that echo through my life
on an endless loop.
My father intones
quoting Longfellow
that life is real! Life is earnest.
While the counterpoint
from my mother
advises
a little nonsense now and then.
Both ring true.
Not bad messages for life.
But sometimes
the earnestness is too earnest
the reality too real.
Then's the time
for mischief. For fun.
For the impulse, the imp
that skips and giggles its way through life
even when it shouldn't.
Especially when it shouldn't.
I hear these two refrains
in stereo sound.
One in my right ear. One in my left.
Though I can hold a hand over one ear
or the other.

Christmas II

Christmas Eve
Mr Johnson brings his truck
He and Dad go
pick up a trestle table
from some hall.
Erect it on the veranda
for us all to sit around tomorrow.
We cut strips of crepe paper.
Fold them into chains
to hang above the table.
The trestle table on the veranda.
We get big blocks of ice
from somewhere.
Put them in the concrete tubs
with the bottles of beer and soft drink.
Cover them with hessian bags.
They'll be cold for tomorrow.
On Christmas Day everyone comes.
Brothers and sisters
nieces and nephews now too
and bring their love.
So much love gathered in one place.
One Christmas morning I start to cry.
I don't know why I am crying
I am not sad. Not really.
I am happy.
But sad too in a strange kind of way
that I don't understand and can't explain.

Maureen teases me.
Says I'm crying
because everyone gave me
soap and talcum powder.
I'm of the age for soap and talcum powder.
No, Maureen. It's not that.
I don't mind the soap and the talcum powder.
Soap and talcum powder are fine.
I think I sense
in the midst of all that love
that something is about to slip away.
Something precious that I cannot grasp.
Cannot hold on to.
I feel it melting already
like the blocks of ice in the tubs.
Melting as I try to keep hold of it.
I think I am mourning
the passing of my childhood
the coming loss of innocence
that only knows this simple. All embracing. Love.
I somehow know
that this too shall pass
And I don't want that.
I want to hold on to it. For ever.
But I know I can't.
I know
I must soon put aside childish things.
And that is why I cry.

The times are a-changing

Time to leave St Ambrose's.
Leave Sister Zita
whose face goes red
whose voice rises
to shrill
as she wields her cane
Which leaves its marks. Its weals. Its welts.
On hands. On legs. On souls.
Time to leave the boys
and their loud rough games.
The boys
who tramp in after lunch
their faces red
like Sister Zita's.
Theirs red and sweaty.
Hair dishevelled.
Shirts pulled out.
Buttons pulled off
from their loud rough games.
Sister Zita has one last message:
'Take care what you read'
She warns.
'Some people read themselves out of the church.'
Some of us don't take care.
Not enough.
The time has come to disperse.
Separate. Go our different ways.
I to All Hallows. A School for Young Ladies.
The school motto in French. *Dieu et Devoir*. God and Duty.

No shrill voices there. No wielded canes.
No frightening tales.
We walk sedately. Two by two.
Up the stairs in silence.
The scent of fresh flowers and beeswax
hanging in the air.
Taught not to fear
but to wonder
at the mysteries of creator and creation.
Taught to think. To question. To achieve.
To set the world aright.
We can do that.
We head towards the 60s.
The world is changing.
I am changing.
I am leaving childhood behind.
I am becoming the person
I am to become.
Finding the answer to the question
Who is she now?

www.ingramcontent.com/pod-product-compliance
Lightning Source LLC
Chambersburg PA
CBHW062142100526
44589CB00014B/1663